Play the Guitar

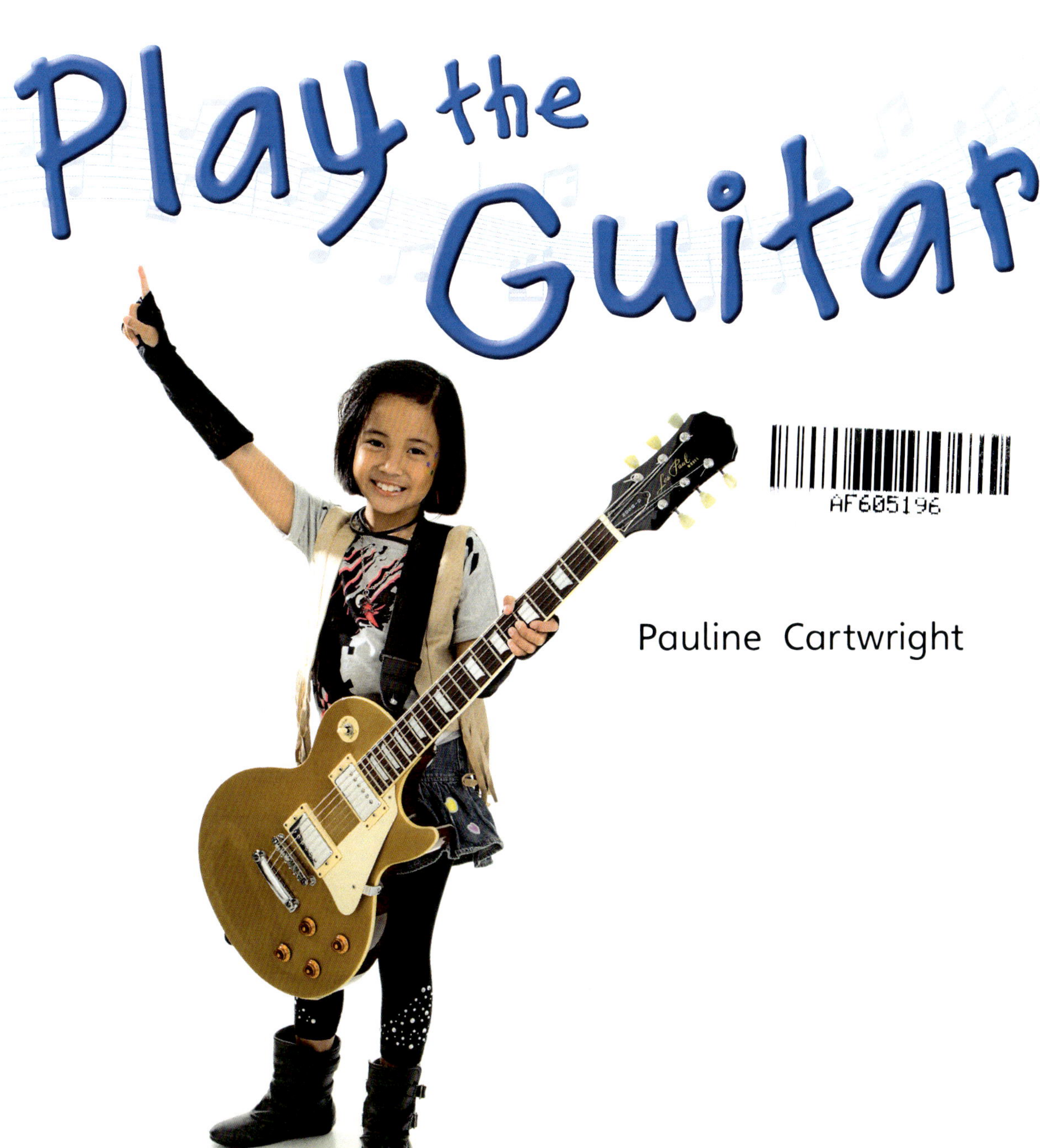

AF605196

Pauline Cartwright

This is a guitar.
You can make music
with a guitar.

Some guitars are little.

Some guitars are big.

A guitar has strings.
Each string makes
a different sound.

You play the guitar with your hands. One hand holds the strings down. One hand plucks the strings.

You can also pluck
the strings with a pick.

You can sit down
to play the guitar.

You can stand up
to play the guitar.

It is fun to play the guitar in a band.

There are three guitars in this band.

You can make your own guitar.
You will need:

Steps

1. Take out the plastic.
2. Take out the tissues!

3 Draw a circle at one end of the box.

4 Ask a grown-up to cut out the circle.

5 Stick the roll in the box.

6 Put a rubber band on this side of the box.

7 Then put a rubber band on this side of the box.

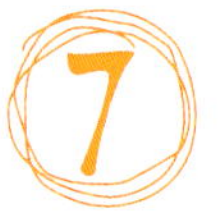

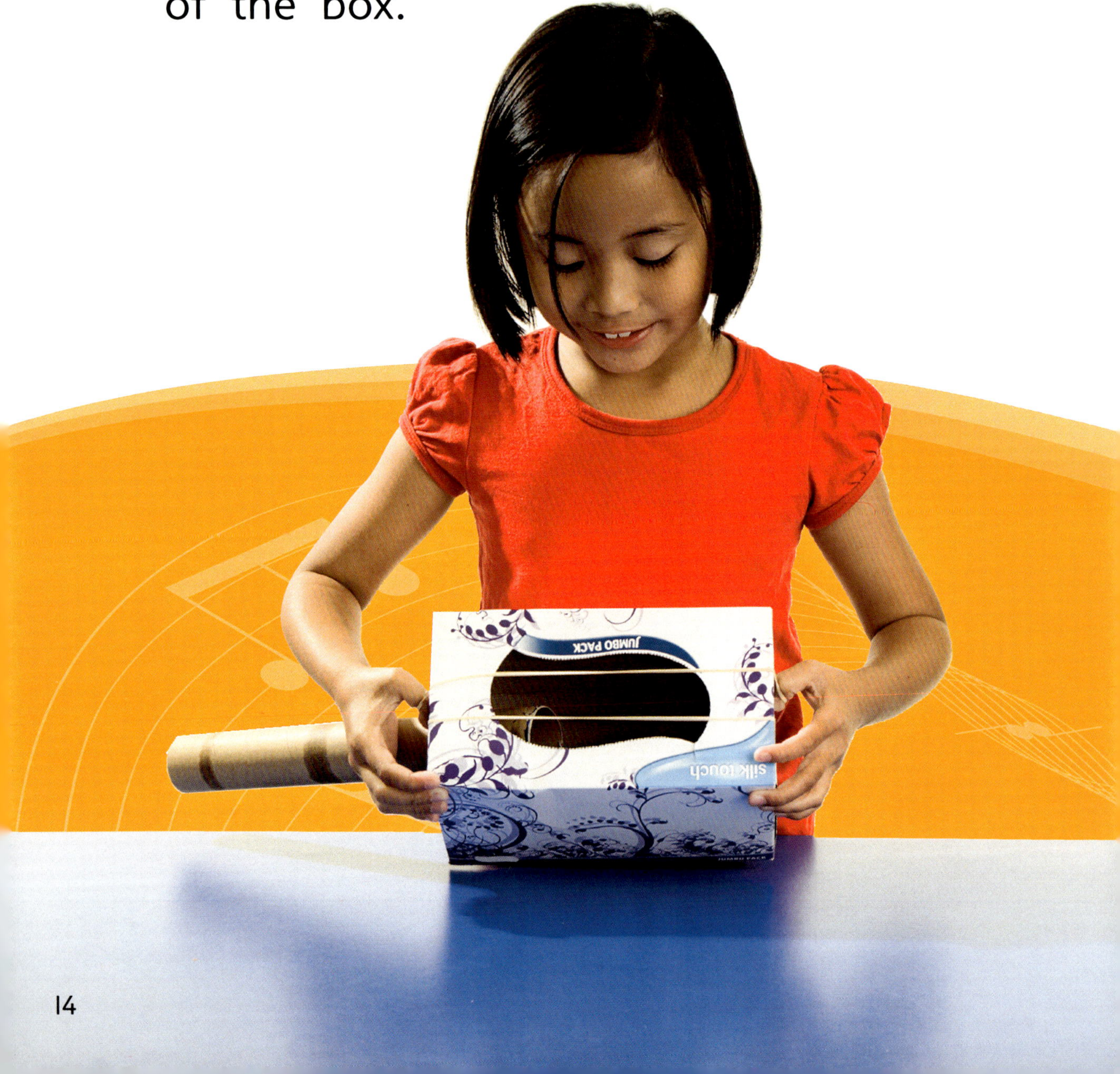

8 Make your guitar look good!

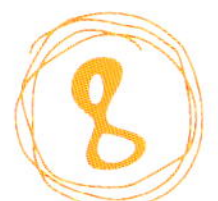

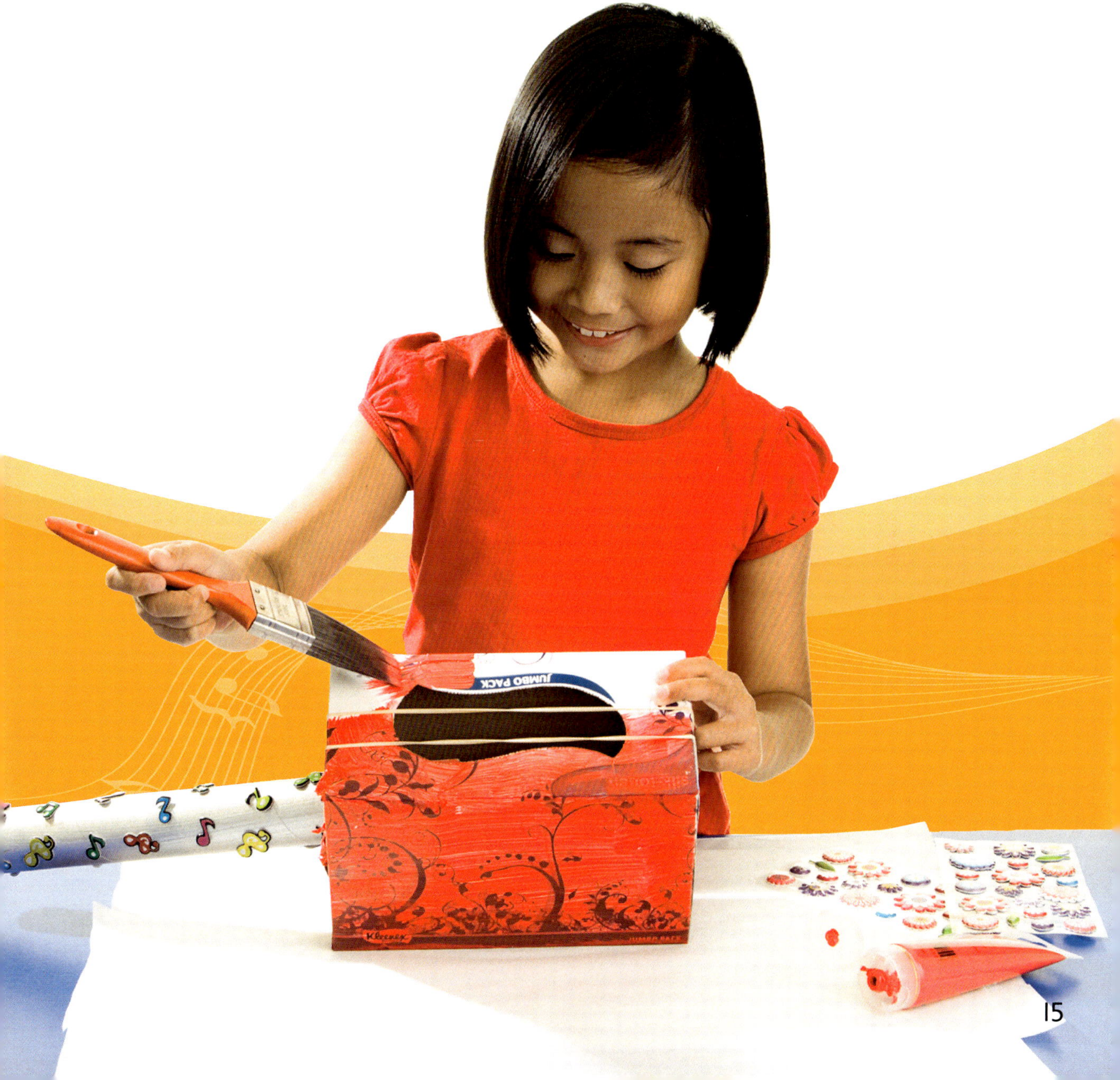

9 Now play your guitar!